POLAR BEARS

DR. TRACEY RICH & ANDY ROUSE

Evans Mitchell Books

Foreword

Recently there has been a lot of publicity about climate change in the Arctic and how it affects polar bears. The Arctic Council and the International Arctic Science Committee, consisting of over 300 scientists and experts from around the world, concluded that we have lost 20% of the sea ice in the Far North in the last two decades. This directly affects polar bears as the sea ice is the platform from which they hunt. The IUCN's Polar Bear Specialist Group has documented a 16% decline in the Western Hudson Bay population in just the last decade. The group predicts the decline will continue over the next 50 years.

Polar Bears International's focus is on conservation through education. Under this umbrella, we sponsor key research projects that directly affect polar bears. We also work hard to develop "Ambassadors of the Arctic" though educational programs that help people to think globally and act locally.

We believe the more that you know about the Far North the more you will appreciate the delicate balance of nature that it possesses. In the following pages you will come to realize the magnitude of the challenges that the polar bear faces every day. It is up to all of us to use this knowledge and motivate others to become better caretakers of this precious planet that we live on.

Robert Buchanan
President of Polar Bears International

POLAR BEARS

Wildlife Monographs – Polar Bears
Copyright © 2006 Evans Mitchell Books

Text and Photography Copyright © 2006
Dr Tracey Rich and Andy Rouse
Reprinted in 2008

Dr Tracey Rich and Andy Rouse have asserted
their rights to be identified as the author and
photographer of this work in accordance with Section
77 of the Copyright, Designs and Patents Act 1988

First published in the United Kingdom in 2007 by:
Evans Mitchell Books
The Old Forge, Forge Mews
16 Church Street
Rickmansworth
Hertfordshire WD3 1DH
United Kingdom
www.embooks.co.uk

Jacket and Book Design by:
Roy Platten
Eclipse
Roy.eclipse@btopenworld.com

British Library Cataloguing in Publication Data.
A CIP record of this book is available
on request from the British Library.

ISBN: 978-1-901268-15-7

Pre Press: F E Burman, London, United Kingdom

Printed in Thailand

Contents

Introduction

Polar Bears are synonymous with the Arctic realm. The great white bear lives in one of the most hostile environments on Earth, surviving in freezing temperatures in excess of -45°C (-49°F) with little shelter. The largest land predator, the polar bear has a fearsome and unfounded reputation for aggression. Far from being an indiscriminate killer, the polar bear lives a fragile existence in one of the last remaining wildernesses on the planet. Living on its wits and dependent upon the miraculous adaptations nature has given it to live, feed and breed in the sub-zero temperatures and howling winds of the pack ice, the polar bear is above all a survivor in locations where we, as humans, fear to tread. Acutely attuned to its environment, the polar bear has been revered by nations for thousands of years and in more recent times, sadly exploited too.

Above: The polar bear, as you can see, is far from being an aggressor.

Opposite page: The polar bear survives in conditions, we as human beings, find intolerable.

Today, threatened as never before, the polar bear faces the greatest-ever challenge to its survival. Will the polar bear be able to cope with a rapidly changing environment and the onset of global warming or could this be the end of one of the most impressive and fascinating mammals on Earth?

Wildlife Monographs – Polar Bears gives us an insight into its world – one with which most of us are unfamiliar. Witnessed by the incredible photography of some of the world's best wildlife photographers, glimpse some of the most intimate moments of a bear's life; emerging for the first time from its den and finding food amidst the Arctic wastelands. Follow the story of the lives of these fascinating creatures and join us in an incredible journey to the kingdom of the ice bear.

Right: Ice, is the key to polar bear survival. What will global climate change mean for the polar bear in the future?

History and Distribution

Polar Bears (*Ursus maritimus*) are found in northern circumpolar areas of the world; areas that are too inhospitable for the majority of the human population to survive with the exception of native peoples on the peripheries. Their existence is tied to the sub-zero temperatures of the polar ice cap and pack ice sheets that migrate around the northern-most reaches of the globe. Principally found north of the Arctic Circle (66°33'N), the modern polar bear is likely to have been found further south than their present day distribution dictates as colder climatic conditions permitted their existence as far south as the coasts of Scandinavia and Newfoundland. The word "Arctic" comes from the Greek "Arkitos" meaning 'country of the Great Bear'. It would be nice to think that the name described the polar bear itself, in fact it describes the Great Bear constellation or Ursus major.

Opposite page: A solitary life on the pack ice.

Above: Polar bear tracks on ice.

Overleaf: The polar bear is believed to have evolved from the brown or grizzly bear in relatively recent times.

The polar bear is a great example of evolution in action; its speciation being incredibly rapid in evolutionary terms and especially for a mammal. The distinct lack of fossil evidence of the polar bear leads palaeontologists to surmise that polar bears have existed as a separate species for a relatively short period of time. Likewise, the areas in which polar bears are found have only recently emerged from the frozen seas. Believed to have been one of the most recently evolved of the world's eight species of bears; the polar bear diverged from the brown bear or grizzly bear *(Ursus arctos)* some 100,000 to 250,000 years ago during the mid-Pleistocene. Originally, the polar bear was larger than the polar bears we see today (approximately 15% larger). It is likely that the modern day polar bear became a separate species as a population of bears gradually became isolated from the Siberian brown bear population by the retreating ice caps caused by a natural warming of the climate. This geographical isolation and subsequent adaptation to the climatic conditions of the Arctic has meant that the polar bear is now restricted only to areas of extreme cold where pack ice and floes exist allowing them to effectively hunt for their prime food resource – the seal.

Above: Living on the pack ice; polar bears became geographically isolated from other bears as the ice cap retreated during natural warming of the world's climate.

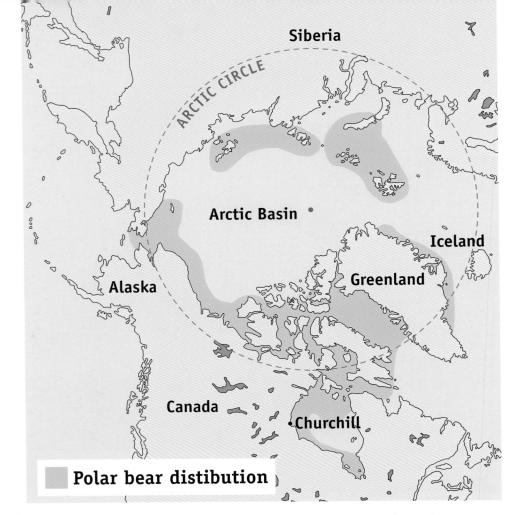

Siberia

ARCTIC CIRCLE

Arctic Basin

Iceland

Greenland

Alaska

Canada

Churchill

Polar bear distibution

The polar bear is a unique species but its population can be divided into six main sub-populations throughout the Arctic region, these being;

1. Canadian Arctic Archipelago (including James and Hudson Bays)

2. Greenland

3. North and North-west Alaska and North-west Canada (Beaufort Sea)

4. Chukchi Sea (including Wrangel Island and Western Alaska)

5. Spitzbergen/Franz Josef Land

6. Central Siberia

There is some debate whether hybridisation of polar and brown bears can occur at the most extreme peripheries of the polar bear's circumpolar range where polar bears become isolated from the pack ice during summer and hence their traditional food resource. It is currently estimated that the world population of polar bears is between 22,000 and 27,000 individuals, spread throughout the circumpolar region.

Distinguishing Features

The polar bear is the most distinctive animal living on the frozen horizons of the High Arctic. The largest land predator on Earth; it is difficult to appreciate the size of a polar bear when you see it amongst the vast, featureless landscape in which it lives. The polar bear is larger than its nearest cousin, the brown bear, despite the fact that it has a considerably smaller and more elongated skull. It does not have the characteristic shoulder hump of the brown bear indeed its haunches are higher than its shoulders giving an overall impression of roundness. Its head is small in comparison to the rest of its bulky body and its ears are also small – a direct adaptation to the extreme cold and characteristic of marine mammals, of which the polar bear, is one.

Opposite page: A small head and ears are characteristic of the polar bear and are adaptations to cold.

Above: A predator: the polar bear has sharp teeth and a profile adapted to hunting.

Its paws are large and are furnished with long, sharp, non-retractable claws used for traction on the snow and ice as well as for hunting purposes when despatching their prey. Their paws measure in the region of 31cm (12ins) across with claws on average about 5.1cm (2ins) long. They also act as snowshoes; spreading the animal's weight across the icy surface. The black pads on the base of the foot are covered in coarse 'papillae' or bumps to assist with grip in the slippery Arctic environment. The paws have slight webbing between their five toes which act as both oars and rudders when swimming. They are also surrounded by long fringes of fur providing further protection from the freezing ground and minimising contact with it and thus heat loss.

The teeth of the polar bear are finer and sharper that those of most other carnivores but are attached via large roots. Polar bear teeth suggest that the animal evolved from a predominantly vegetarian omnivore to a more carnivorous diet providing further support for the theory of its evolution from the brown bear; a species common throughout lower latitudes of the northern hemisphere.

Above: Walking on ice can be slippery. The bear's large paws are designed to give grip as well as being used in water as paddles.

Opposite page and overleaf: Large paws and teeth are also useful when competing with others. The predominantly white coat of the bear can appear in a variety of different shades.

Polar bear males are significantly larger than females. A male polar bear can reach 2.5–3m (8–10ft) in length or when standing on their hind legs, whilst the female is 1.9–2.5m (6–8ft) in length. Their weight fluctuates throughout the year with variations in food sources and availability. On average an adult male will weigh between 250–770kg (550–1700lbs) and the female less than half this, 90–320kg (200–700lbs). Although not immediately apparent, the polar bear does have a tail which is usually hidden under its thick coat. The tail can reach 33cm (13ins) in length in males and around 16cm (6ins) in females.

Above: The polar bear is the largest land predator in the Arctic.

Opposite page, top: Small, low set ears are a response to the cold environment, minimizing heat loss.

Opposite page, bottom: The bear's coat colour and profile assists hunting in Arctic habitats.

Thermoregulation

The coat of the polar bear is probably one of its most distinguishing features. During its evolution, it is likely that the bears' white coat conferred significant hunting and survival advantages living on pack ice. Over time these bears would breed more successfully in these areas than their darker counterparts, and coupled with geographical isolation the species became distinct from the rest of the bear population.

The 'white' coat is a result of the lack of pigmentation within the hair shaft; in fact each hair is a hollow tube, the white colour appearing only as a result of reflective light. Interestingly, the polar bear does not show up under infra-red light, clearly demonstrating the amazing insulating qualities of their coat.

It has been suggested that the hollow nature of the hair shaft may concentrate warming ultra-violet light down to the epidermis or outer layer of the skin although scientific evidence is inconclusive. The coat colour can vary from the almost pure and fresh whites of the polar bear cubs to a distinctly yellow or orange-tinged pelage. A dirty yellow-coloured coat is often seen during the summer months as bears spend less time in water and are exposed to increased sunlight. The fur may also become stained by oils from the bear, its food and pollutants.

The polar bear's coat is a key to its survival in the polar environment. It comprises two distinct layers. The layer closest to the skin is made up of short, soft and densely packed hairs. This traps a layer of air against the skin which becomes heated by the body and works as an insulating layer. On top lie the guard hairs which are less densely packed and are coarse in texture. The effect of wind-chill can be significant in the Arctic environment, sometimes doubling the effect of cold on an object; the guard hairs assist in dissipating water, snow and ice and ensure sufficient wind-proofing from the ferocious gales that whip across the Arctic landscape.

Right: The double-layered coat is one of the bear's main adaptations to survival in such harsh and cold conditions.

Overleaf, left: Fat or blubber layers also protect the bear from the cold. A day bed can protect the bear from the effects of wind-chill.

Overleaf, right, top: Conserving heat is fine when conditions are cold. When warm, a bear may stretch out on the ice to cool down.

Overleaf, right, middle: A relatively slow pace of life means that bears can live till around 15 years old.

Overleaf, right, bottom: Sleeping and inactivity also conserve energy and heat.

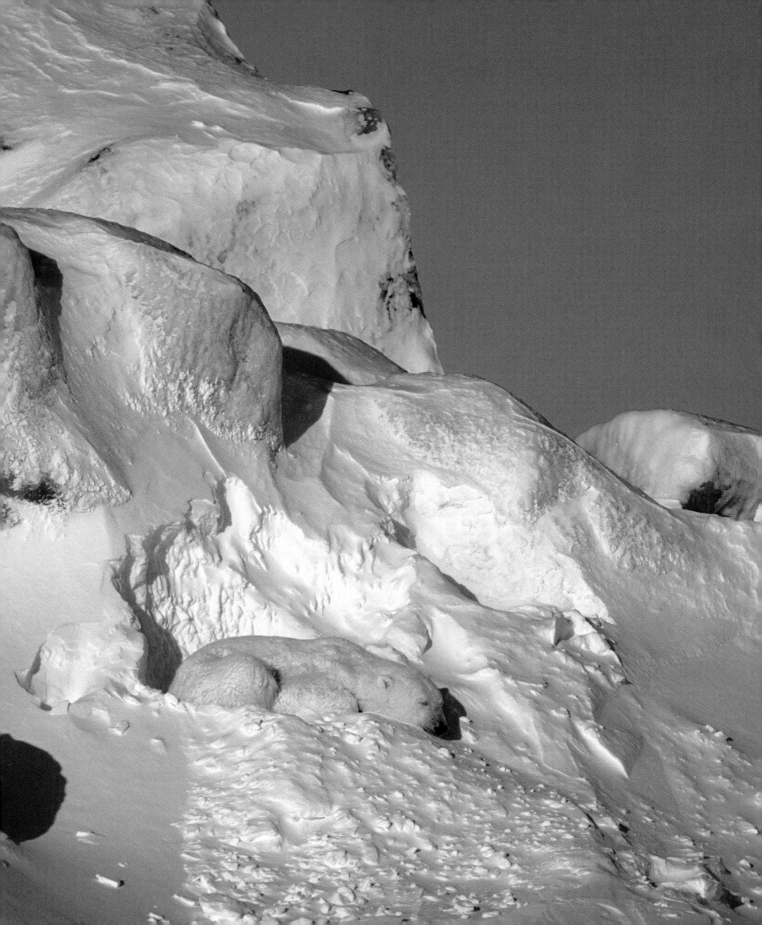

The depth of insulation and the length of hair shafts vary according to season. The hairs become shorter (around 3cm/1.2ins of insulating layer and 5cm/2ins length of guard hairs) and more yellow during the summer. In winter, the coat becomes thicker, longer (5–6cm/2–2.5ins of insulation and 8cm/3ins guard hairs) and whiter. Likewise, the depth of the fur varies across the body, being shorter along the back and longer on the belly. In order to maintain these vital insulating and waterproofing qualities of the bear's coat, they fastidiously clean themselves at every opportunity. After feeding, they pay a great deal of attention to every area of their fur including the removal of balled ice and snow between their paws. A dirty coat can quickly lead to hypothermia and death in such a harsh environment.

The polar bear's skin is pigmented with melanin giving it a dark, almost black colouration. The dark colour assists the retention of heat close to the body from the insulating layer of fur. Directly under the skin, the polar bear has a deep layer of fat/blubber, some 11.5cm (4.5ins) thick. This provides the most efficient means of storing energy over a prolonged period of time as well as supplying the animal with a super-effective means of insulation against the biting cold sub-zero temperatures it experiences. The fat layer is deposited during times when there is a glut of high-calorie food such as seals.

A specialised system of heat-exchange within the bear's respiratory and circulation systems ensures that heat is not wasted but is conserved within the body and reduces the energy needed to warm such a large mammal within such a cold environment. The temperature of the polar bear is average for mammals of all kinds (37°C/98.6°F). Prolonged periods of inactivity also serve to retain heat and conserve vital fat and energy reserves. A resting bear utilises 13 times less energy than one that is active.

Although the polar bear has highly specialised physical and physiological mechanisms to retain heat, they face difficulties of being too hot during any form of exercise. Should a polar bear exert too much energy, perhaps during hunting or fleeing, it can quickly overheat. Consequently, bears rarely run of their own choice. The bear's only other means of losing heat is to pant in a similar manner to a dog, swim, or to try to lose heat by lying spread-eagled on the ice or tundra. Polar bears also 'wash' themselves in snow and ice in attempts to cool themselves and can become severely stressed when too hot.

The life of a polar bear occurs at a reasonably slow pace and thus they are long-lived in mammalian terms. Their average life span in the wild is between 15–18 years of age although they can live for almost double this in captivity. They have a low mortality of only 5% per year, with starvation being the main cause of death. The polar bears' greatest enemy is the environment followed by other bears, potentially the wolf and Man.

Opposite page, top: Bears keep their coats immaculately clean to maintain its vital insulation properties.

Opposite page, bottom and overleaf: The bears' greatest enemy is the environment.

Habitat and Diet

The High Arctic is the principal realm of the polar bear and its climate is the predominant force governing the lives of the bears. The polar bear habitat is sometimes likened to a desert albeit at the colder extremes of the world's climate than the hottest. In common with the desert, there is no vegetation except on the peripheral snow-covered tundra or permafrost in coastal areas.

Despite first impressions, the pack ice is not just a blank canvas of snow and ice. The ice is constantly on the move due to currents, tidal movements, the actions of constant freezing and thawing and fluctuating temperatures throughout the year. These movements create some spectacular scenery from country-sized icebergs and mountains of snow and ice, to deep crevices, cracks, textured ice resembling the frozen waves of the sea, deep fissures and snow drifts. Howling winds and snow storms are a common daily occurrence.

Above: The Arctic landscape is a patchwork of ice and snow sculptures.

Opposite page: Bears may spend several hours if not days waiting for the chance to hunt.

So, if the Arctic really is so inhospitable what do polar bears manage to find to eat? Seals are the essential component of the polar bear's diet although this is supplemented by local variations according to season. Being restricted to the pack ice and margins of tundra during summer, the polar bear has a significantly reduced variety of potential food resources. Few other animal species can survive in the high latitudes of the northern hemisphere and especially those which are of sufficient calorific value and quantity to sustain such an enormous mammal.

The predominant species of seal chosen as prey by polar bears is dependent upon the sub-population and location in which individual bears live. The seal species that is without doubt the most important and most frequently consumed by the polar bear is the Ringed Seal *(Phoca hispida)*. The ringed seal population is estimated to be between six and seven million individuals each reaching a weight of between 60–100kg (132–220lbs). It is a prolific breeder and is often the only suitable prey to sustain the energy needs of the polar bear, thus their survival and population fluctuations are inextricably linked with the survival of the polar bear. In other regions, the less prolific Bearded Seal *(Erignathus barbatus)*, Common Seal *(Phoca vitullina)*, Harp Seal *(Pagophiius groenlandicus)*, Hooded Seal *(Cristophora cristata)* and even Walrus *(Odobenus rosmarus)* are taken when they become locally abundant or when opportunity arises.

Throughout the year, the polar bears' diet fluctuates with the presence and absence of seals and their density in particular areas. Their lifestyle is one of 'fast and feast'; at times bears will gorge themselves on plentiful food supplies whilst at others they will resort to eating birds, chicks and their eggs (comprising upto 60% of the diet in summer), kelp, lichens, salmon, mussels and clams, lemmings, musk rat and even reindeer when times are lean. Infrequently featuring on the list of food items are beached or trapped whales that wash up along the coastlines or have become trapped in the fast moving ice. Carrion is also taken if food supplies are scarce. When food is scarce in summer months, polar bears may enter a state known as 'walking hibernation'. At this time the bears will spend considerable amounts of time sleeping and conserving their energy. Contrary to popular thought, the polar bear does not technically hibernate in winter. Females do spend several months in a carefully excavated den during the winter when giving birth to young where body temperature and metabolism are reduced but males and non-gestating females do not.

Opposite page, top: Bears wander the ice in search of food.

Opposite page, middle: Bear in frozen kelp bed at end of summer.

Opposite page, bottom: Bears come into contact with each other when waiting for pack ice to form.

Above: Bear sniffing seals beneath ice.

Overleaf, left, top: Polar bears are active hunters.

Overleaf, left, bottom: Bears can swim very well and are classified as marine mammals.

Overleaf, right: Bears are constantly searching the sea ice for food.

At lean times, polar bears scavenge in a similar manner to other bears (even from human rubbish dumps) but the polar bears' main means of acquiring food is through actively hunting their prey. During winter, seals are obliged to maintain a set of breathing holes at breaks or leads in the ice or by cutting their own in the frozen surface of the sea. The seals visit some 10–15 holes on a regular patrolling route. The polar bear is a patient and yet determined hunter, it will lie in wait downwind of the seal's breathing hole for several hours, if not days, before choosing the precise moment to make its strike; attacking its chosen prey as it surfaces. The kill involves a swift bite to the head and is often preceded by a swift wipe with the fore paw which may stun and even kill the prey directly. The prey is often dragged far from the site of the kill (up to 3 km/1.8miles) thus avoiding the attention of competitors and finding more stable ground.

Top left: Hunting for seals.

Top right: Bear waiting by seal hole.

Middle left: Bear pouncing on seal den.

Middle right: Bear climbing from seal hole (failed hunting attempt).

Bottom:Bear with seal carcass.

Opposite page: Harp seal pup.

As spring approaches, seals give birth to their young inside snow caves or dens excavated from the snow drift covering their breathing holes in land-fast ice. At this rather sedentary time (of up to 2 months), the seal and its young are vulnerable. On the surface, the seal's breathing holes are covered by a layer of packed snow forming a small hummock or dome in the snow surface. It is here that the bear concentrates its hunting efforts. The polar bear, guided by its super effective sense of smell, can detect an occupied den, listening for the tell-tale noises of the seal pulling itself from the freezing waters below. It strikes by rearing upon its hind legs and with its full weight crashes down on top of the snow dome, breaking into the den and snatching the young.

Most adult seals escape into the water but the young are much slower and inexperienced; many will become prey for the bears. In early summer, when concealment is no longer a viable hunting technique, the polar bear may simply resort to stalking their resting prey, charging from a distance of around 20m (66ft) and/or pouncing from as close as 6.1m (20ft). Legend has it that the polar bear will cover its nose with its paw when waiting in ambush of a seal but in reality there is little evidence for this. Bears that are thwarted in their attempts at hunting are often known to take their aggression out on the local environment, scuffing and throwing snow and ice and also slapping the ground leading to another local legend – that polar bears kill seals by throwing snowballs at them!

When feeding, the polar bear will preferentially consume the fat and brain from the carcass. The cholesterol levels of polar bears have been found to drop following feeding due to the Omega 3 fish oils contained within the seal fat. On average, a feeding session will last for 30 minutes, eating up to 20% of their body weight (50–154kg/110–340lbs) in a single sitting, followed by 15 minutes cleaning or bathing and then a 4–5 hour siesta before moving on. Research has shown that polar bears will eat about 6 seals per month for 6 months of the year. The polar bear, when satiated, will (unlike other bear species) often leave the remnants of its kill for other scavengers such as the Arctic Fox *(Alopex lagopus)* and gulls. As these scavengers are dependent upon the successful hunting of the bears, it has been suggested that they have a symbiotic relationship although there is no scientific evidence to support this.

Above: A scavenger, the arctic fox will follow bears for the remains of their kills.

Opposite page, top: Females with young cubs may not feed for several months.

Opposite page, bottom: A bear will rest after feeding.

Overleaf: A bear can walk for many miles in search of food.

Social Structure and Communication

Norwegians use the term "The rider of icebergs", which aptly describes the social structure of the polar bear that we know today. The polar bear is not a particularly social animal and spends much of its life in isolation from other bears only coming together when resources, either food or mates, dictate. By following the migration of its food sources caused by the thawing and freezing of ice floes throughout the year the polar bear is unable to defend its resources and is thus not territorial and home ranges often overlap. The range over which polar bears move is largely dependent upon available resources, some may wander many hundreds of kilometres whilst others remain reasonably sedentary when resources are plentiful. In general, polar bears are found within 80km (50 miles) of the coastline, the exact position of which changes with the extension and reduction in the pack ice.

Opposite page: Polar bears wrestle to determine dominance.

Above: Young bear sniffing scent mark.

Polar bears' favoured means of locomotion is a loping walk. They are constantly 'on the move' and travel incessantly in search of resources. The bears tend to take the most direct route possible and few obstacles prove difficult for a bear to overcome. The bear will zigzag constantly in an attempt to search out potential food or mates. Quartering is a well-known behaviour in many mammals and is used to assess and locate the source of a particular scent. The speed at which they travel can be maintained for considerable periods of time (approximately 4–6kph/2.5–3.7mph). For brief periods they can reach speeds on average 25kph (15.5mph) when running.

Top: Polar bear investigating scent in the air.

Above: Polar bear urine is also used as a "scent mark" to communicate with others.

In addition to travel on land and ice, the polar bear, as one may expect from a marine mammal, is an expert swimmer covering distances of up to 100km (62 miles) at an average speed of 10 kph (6 mph). Bears are also able to achieve dives of up to 5m (16.5ft) holding their breath for a period of up to 2 minutes; their rear feet being used as rudders. They are able to see underwater too, up to 4.6m (15ft). Their significant subcutaneous fat layer also works as a buoyancy aid in the water. The waterproofing afforded to the animal from its coat prevents the bear's skin coming into direct contact with the freezing waters but once back on land the bear will rapidly shake excess water from its coat; re-establishing maximal insulting properties of the fur for the prevailing conditions found on land.

Despite a principally solitary lifestyle, the polar bear has a complex array of senses tailored to life in a vast and reasonably featureless environment. The bear's eyesight is believed to be similar to that of human beings but has a specialised membrane covering the eye, protecting it from "snow-blindness" that can be experienced from reflected light from the surroundings. It also protects the eye from small particles of snow and ice present in the violent winds of the Arctic and when swimming underwater. Their eyesight is particularly good at detecting movement which is important in a vast, homogeneous environment where proportion and distance is difficult to assess.

Top: Polar bears have a ritualized greeting ceremony involving posturing and touching jaws.

The polar bear's hearing is also similar to our own. Noise in the Arctic is mostly a result of the wind and movement of ice, except when bears meet and between mother and her young. Consequently, acoustic communication is most effective over shorter distances and in intimate circumstances.

The dominant sense of the polar bear is smell. In a pristine environment devoid of pollutants and with constant wind, scent can travel over vast distances uninterrupted. The scent reaches the bear intact and thus provides a valuable source of information about the originator. A polar bear is able to smell a seal beneath the ice and can also detect females in oestrus from a distance of several tens of kilometres. The bear possesses the 'Jacobson organ' which is a gland located at the beginning of the respiratory tract and is familiar in many carnivorous animals. The gland is believed to heighten the perception of smells and tastes, therefore demonstrating the importance of smell to the polar bear and its suitability to the Arctic environment. The tongue is used to taste objects and bears can often be seen flicking their tongue on approach to an unfamiliar object, presumably tasting the air and drawing moisture over the Jacobson organ.

This page and opposite, bottom: Adult polar bears have little physical contact; when they do interact a strict hierarchy develops through posturing and wrestling.

Tactile communication is useful to the polar bear in its exploration of the environment. Bears use their teeth, tongue, lips and paws to touch and assess novel objects. They will often use their weight to test the firmness of objects and areas of ice by carefully treading upon it. On patches of thin ice, bears are known to crawl, thus spreading their weight.

It remains unknown how polar bears navigate amongst the featureless and vast areas of the Arctic. It has been suggested that in addition to their heightened sense of smell and possible use of prevailing winds and currents within the ice floes, the polar bear has some capacity to detect moisture in the atmosphere such as clouds and humidity which lead them towards the edges of the pack ice and fruitful hunting grounds.

Top: Three bears interacting when gathering for sea ice to form.

Complex body language is important to communication between bears. Upon meeting another bear, it is clear that a strict hierarchy develops between individuals and that this is based upon physical strength, age, sex, and reproductive status of the individuals. In general, the hierarchy comprises of adult males, followed by adult females, adult females without young, sub-adults and young. This determines each individual's priority to access of the particular resource, e.g. food.

Posturing is the means by which bears assess each other. A greeting comprises a nose to nose posture whilst circling signifies begging behaviour and is exhibited most frequently by subordinate animals. Submissive bears will always remain downwind of a more dominant individual. In conjunction with body postures, polar bears have a repertoire of growls, hisses, roars and squeaks which tell others of their anger and aggression, defence, stress or desire to play or court another. Aggression is signalled by the lowering of the head, ears laid flat against the head combined with growling, hissing and snorting. Play is initiated by wagging the head from side to side or standing on the hind legs with the chin pressed against the chest.

Top: Outright aggression between bears is rare. Tests of dominance and play are common when individuals come together.

Right: The sense of smell is predominant in the world of the polar bear; assisting finding both food and mates.

Minor displays of aggression between bears are frequent when in close proximity; most being between equally matched males and from females defending their young. True aggression or fighting, is, as in most animals, avoided at all costs. In serious encounters a bear will give a number of warnings to a challenger before engaging in a fight. The warnings consist of aggressive growls, head shaking, snarls and clacking of the jaws and teeth which are usually enough to extinguish the challenge. True aggression involves the use of teeth and claws as weapons and can lead to serious injury and potential death. Mock fighting or wrestling between young males is frequent in summer and often involve rearing on their hind legs and pushing with the forelegs in attempts to assert dominance. Young females avoid other bears, especially males, preferring to remain as far as possible from them.

Top left: Females with cubs avoid males if possible.

Top right: Mock fighting can be highly energetic.

Opposite page:Bears may stand on their hind legs to get a better view or sniff at an unfamiliar object or individual.

Overleaf:Polar bear playing in the snow.

Reproduction and Growing Up

Female polar bears reach sexual maturity at the age of 4 or 5 years and can remain reproductively active until the age of 27 years (although longer in captivity). They are unlikely to have their first set of cubs until they are between 5 and 6 years old, reaching their optimal reproductive success around 14 to 16 years old. Males also become sexually active at the age of 5 years but do not mate successful until they are between 8 and 10 years old. This is principally a result of competition between males; larger and stronger bears are the most successful sires. On average there are 3 males to every available female polar bear without dependents.

Female polar bears attain the state of oestrus at a time between mid-March and the beginning of May, depending on their physical condition, latitude and prevailing weather conditions. They remain in oestrus for a period of 4 weeks during which time males active seek them. Males reach their maximum reproductive peak during April until the end of July.

Opposite page: Around the age of 2–3 years, polar bear cubs must leave the comfort of their mother, to fend for themselves.

Above: Females reach their optimum reproductive state at around 14 years of age.

Overleaf: A courting couple.

Upon entering oestrus, female polar bears cease eating. They are seen to urinate frequently thus advertising their reproductive state to all males in the vicinity. Males in turn are seen to counter-mark her signals, advertising their intentions and inviting others to investigate the current situation. Likewise, they will give off 'pheromones', miniscule chemicals that will travel on the wind and be detected by males downwind.

The process of courtship involves a protracted series of chasing and games between the courting couple. The male appears nervous and can often be seen with an extended tongue hanging from his mouth. He incessantly follows the female wherever she goes, whining and mewing after her. He defends his chosen female from any other suitors and steers her away from other bears.

The pair will remain together for a week and will copulate frequently. Studies in captivity have shown that this lasts for around 30 minutes. Towards the end of the female's period of oestrus, she becomes increasingly promiscuous in an attempt to improve her chances of a successful fertilization. Once this period has ended the female bear sets out on a quest to find food. Her mission is to gain as much weight as possible during the spring and summer before she enters her winter den. A female polar bear needs to be at least 150kg (330lbs) to ensure that both she and her cubs will survive the winter in their den.

Top and opposite page:
Courtship between male
and female...

...can last for days...

...and days...

At the end of the summer, pregnant females search out an area suitable for constructing their winter den; the place where she will give birth and look after her offspring until the following spring. The den itself is a very simple chamber approximately 2m (6.6ft) by 6m (20ft) and 0.6m (2ft) tall. Located inland and well away from the areas frequented by males; the den is often found in a sheltered area, perhaps near some scarce vegetation and in a snow covered bank where protection from the prevailing weather is maximised. The den's entrance is usually sited facing south to make the most of the spring sunshine when it arrives.

Opposite page: ...until...

Top: After mating the bears go their separate ways.

Overleaf: Female bears can spend 7 or 8 months in their den before emerging with their young.

63

In common with a number of other mammals, such as seals and some deer, the polar bear undergoes delayed implantation of the developing embryo. Despite mating in spring, the development of the pregnancy is stalled until the autumn as the bear enters her den. This means that the young do not begin to develop until conditions are conducive to a successful pregnancy and allows the female bear to conserve her energy reserves for the winter period when they are most needed.

Top: Cubs are tiny when they first emerge and are carefully guarded by their mother.

Opposite page: Despite being small, cubs have to follow their mothers over long distances.

Two months after entering the den, the female gives birth to her young. Normally, polar bears give birth to two offspring and occasionally three. At birth a polar bear cub is naked, blind and weighs on average just 500g (20oz). They quickly migrate towards one of the four nipples and begin suckling safe in the warmth of the mother's insulting fur. Scientific research has shown that the interior of the den may be some 21°C (70°F) warmer than the outside temperature. The female's milk is extremely thick and rich. Its content is 33% fat rising to 46% when the female begins eating seal again in later months.

By comparison, human breast milk contains approximately 4% fat. Needless to say, young cubs develop rapidly and one month after birth, open their eyes. Teeth appear between one and a half and two months at which time, the young begin to explore the den. Their excrement is buried by their mother who keeps the den meticulously clean. Also at this time, the female begins to excavate the den creating a ventilation hole which gradually lowers the internal temperature of the den towards that of the outside and acclimatises the bears to the lower temperatures they will experience when they eventually leave.

During the 7 or 8 months spent in the den, the female does not eat or drink surviving only on her fat reserves built during the preceding summer. Polar bears do not hibernate but reduce their metabolism by half; lowering their heart rate, breathing and body temperature. The normal temperature of a polar bear is the same as other mammals 37°C (98.6°F) but during her stay in the den the female's body temperature can reduce to 35°C (95°F).

As spring approaches (late February – start April), the mother and her young take their first steps outside of the den. This is the first time that the female will have been outside in 26 weeks. Older and younger mothers enter their dens earlier and exit later than others – the timing of which is largely dependent upon the individual's physical condition. For the first few days or weeks, the mother and her young will remain in the vicinity of the den; the young discovering their new world and acclimatising to the Arctic environment.

Top: Occasionally, females will give birth to three young, but this is rare.

Top right: A female normally has two cubs.

Opposite page, bottom: The young will whine and squeak, demanding to be suckled.

The female polar bear is, by this point in time, driven by hunger to move as rapidly as possible with her offspring towards the pack ice and food. A female polar bear may lose almost half of her body weight during gestation and the initial period with her newborns in the den. After several months of fasting, this instinct is essential if both she and her young are to survive. The journey is long and treacherous with such small progeny and their progression is slow; the cubs having to rest frequently. The young cubs carefully follow in the footprints of their mother forming a nose to tail line in the snow. In inclement weather, the mother will shelter her young and even build a temporary snow cave to shelter in if needs be. The need to gain access to food is urgent and cubs that are unable to keep up with the pace or fall ill are left behind. The death rate of cubs in their first year varies between 10 and 35%, the majority being in the first few days outside of the maternal den.

Opposite page, top: Cubs follow carefully in their mother's footprints.

Opposite page, bottom: Frequent rest is essential for tiny legs.

Top left: Cubs are keen to explore the wider world but will stay close to their mother.

Top right: Snuggling in the fur of their mother ensures that cubs stay warm.

Cubs will also take time to play, performing mock battles and charges at each other and their mother and are often seen to ride on their mother's back. The female will continue to suckle her young from time to time during rest periods. Suckling of the young cubs continues until they are 20 months. Vocalisations between mother and cubs are frequent; a combination of squeaks, squeals, whines and growls. The female bear is attentive to the needs of her offspring showing great tenderness with such tiny cubs which remain in contact with her at all times.

Opposite page, top:
Bear families will rest in
sheltered areas for the night.

Opposite page, bottom:
Any areas of shelter are
taken advantage of.

Top: Cubs often play by riding
on their mother's backs.

Bottom:Their mother is a
convenient toy.

During the first year of life the cubs begin to learn all of the skills needed as an adult polar bear in the Arctic. They accompany their mother on hunting expeditions and watch her intently, gaining their first taste of meat following the eruption of molar teeth by the age of 11 months. They begin to attempt hunting postures and techniques themselves during their second year. Learning to hunt becomes the cubs' preoccupation, the youngsters following their mother's daily rhythm and copying everything she does. The bear family avoid other bears if at all possible and especially males. Male polar bears, like some other mammals, are known to kill and eat the cubs of others (infanticide).

Previous page: For the first year, polar bear families are constantly on the move towards food sources.

Top: Learning is achieved by mimicking everything their mother does.

Opposite page, top left: Year-old polar bear cubs.

Opposite page, top right: Cub peering from beneath mother's belly.

Opposite page, bottom: Cubs continue to suckle from their mother whenever possible.

A landmark in the life of the polar bear occurs around the age of 2½ years. At this time, cubs will have grown to a size and learned sufficient lessons in hunting to survive alone. The time of weaning and separation from the mother occurs at various ages depending upon the individual's location and local food abundance. Where plentiful food supplies are available weaning may occur more rapidly and where conditions are harsh, such as in the High Arctic they may remain with the mother until the age of 3 years. This is a tough time for young polar bears whose inexperience can make hunting difficult and many will go hungry. It is crucial at this time that the young bears gain sufficient weight and fat to allow them to survive the winter, not doing so may mean death. Starvation is the biggest cause of death in sub-adult polar bears. After separation, a young bear must make its own way in the world and set up its own home range away from its mother. Young bears have been known to travel more than 1000km (620 miles) to set up home ranges distant from their natal area.

Right: Being alert starts
at an early age.

Man and Polar Bears

Man's relationship with the polar bear has existed for millennia; ancient peoples existing in harmony alongside the bears and alternately becoming both predator and prey. The ancestors of the modern day Inuit and other native communities lived alongside the animals of the Arctic and their lives were inextricably linked to that of their environment and the Arctic's supreme predator. Polar bears were hunted in a sustainable manner and the bears became a significant figure in the folklore and spiritual beliefs of people living throughout the Arctic region from Siberia to Svalbard; Greenland to Alaska.

In many native beliefs, the polar bear was a revered adversary and as such was treated with respect, often commanding the treatment reserved for family members such as fathers, brothers and cousins. The spirit of the ice bear was a powerful force. The skull and fur of the polar bear remained in the home of the hunter and amulets signifying good health and faithfulness were carved from their bones.

Opposite page: Polar bears are threatened by rising global temperatures leading to changes in their habitat.

Above: Road sign in the "polar bear capital of the world", Churchill, Canada.

Traditionally, all parts of the bear kill were used or offered as sacrifice. Skin was used as clothing, bones for tools, fat was eaten as was the tongue but the flesh was seldom, if ever, eaten due to the potential for it to contain parasites and the liver due to its toxicity, the flesh would sometimes be fed to the native peoples' dogs. Live bears also became a valuable commodity and were traded between Scandinavian nations as well as being given as gifts to royalty and the church as ancient documents describe.

Top: Adolescent polar bears are the usual suspects when bears are found in town.

Opposite page, top: Polar bears are revered by many nations and are frequently depicted in art.

Opposite page, bottom:Churchill, Canada.

It was not until the Arctic region was plundered by whalers and began to be discovered by European explorers, intent on finding maritime routes between the leading trading nations of the day, that polar bears were encountered by others nationalities. Ignorant of the native peoples' relationship with the polar bear, the animals became stigmatised and acquired a fearsome reputation for aggression and as potential man-killers. Returning explorers would recount tales of their heroism and bravery in the face of the Arctic and its dangers, thus perpetuating an image of the polar bear which was far from the truth.

The explorers' view of the polar bear was in direct opposition to that of the native peoples of the Arctic who treated the wildlife which shared their home, with respect. The hunting of polar bears became a challenging 'sport', a symbol of status and of Man's ability to conquer even the most inhospitable and inaccessible parts of the globe. Many thousands of polar bears were killed in the process, upsetting the once natural balance that existed between Man and bear in the Arctic. Furthermore, bears were taken from the wild in large numbers to show others in the explorers' home countries and were exhibited in zoological collections throughout the western world.

The polar bear was first scientifically classified by Phipps in 1774 but it was not until the 1900s that the hunting of the bears waned and people began to appreciate the natural magnificence of the Arctic polar region, and the fascinating lives of the people and wildlife living there. Continuous exploration and scientific study followed and gradually the Arctic region and the polar bear in particular, became internationally recognised as requiring special protection. In 1973, the International Agreement on the Conservation of Polar Bears was ratified by the five polar bear nations; Canada, Russia, Norway, Greenland (Denmark) and the United States. This agreement recognised the countries' commitments to conserving the polar bear by restricting its hunting and the trafficking of hides whilst supporting the acquisition and dissemination of knowledge about its ecology and its needs.

The Polar Bear Today

Today, the polar bear remains under threat. The main problems it faces are not from direct hunting pressures which are strictly limited to the basic needs of the native people still living, as their ancestors did, in the Arctic regions of the world. The principal threats to the continued existence of the polar bear come from more indirect sources; pollution, the effects of accelerated global warming; exploitation of natural resources such as oil as well as those associated with increasing human development.

The alterations to the world's climate through the accelerated effects of the global warming (caused by the burning of fossil fuels, destruction of rainforests and the unsustainable lives of modern Man) potentially pose the greatest challenge to the survival of the polar bear in modern times. With a warmer and more unpredictable world climate, ice caps have begun to melt making the pack ice too unstable for bears to hunt upon. Loss of weight and disturbance to reproductive cycles are already being seen and the carefully-balanced Arctic ecosystem has become disrupted. A recent study in 1999 has concluded that 10% fewer polar bear cubs have been born in the Hudson Bay region than were born 20 years before. The future of the polar bear is in some doubt and the species could be extinct in the wild by the end of the twenty-first century with a 30% decline in the population forecast in the next 30–50 years.

Opposite page and above:
A tranquilized female polar bear and cubs being airlifted to safety.

Overleaf: What will the future hold for the polar bear and its fragile Arctic environment?

It is difficult to understand that pollution could be a problem in what may appear to be one of the most pristine habitats on Earth. Miles upon miles of frozen ice and snow are unlikely to be affected by human habitation and its industries concentrated in urban cities – or are they? The Arctic is affected by the everyday lives of all of us, no matter where we live in the world. Tides and prevailing winds arrive in the North and with them bring minute pollutant particles that are trapped in the sea and ice and also in the living organisms it supports. Pollutants include; organochlorides, heavy metals such as lead and mercury, hydrocarbons, benzenes and other small particulate matter commonly used throughout the world for agriculture and to combat pests.

Being at the very top of the food chain, the polar bear is the end point at which all of these pollutants arrive. Biopsies of living polar bears throughout the polar range have shown dramatically high levels of pollutants in their tissues. Levels increase from 2ppm (parts per million) to 20ppm in a west to east gradient from Alaska to Svalbard.

Opposite page: Eco-tourism allows us a privileged view of these magnificent animals.

The reproduction of seals and sea lions are known to be affected by even small levels of pollutants; the levels found in female polar bears in the last decade are several times higher. The pollutants are further concentrated in the polar bear by its fasting during gestation. The gradual use of energy reserves over time concentrate the pollutants further within the body.

Not all areas in the Arctic are devoid of human development and hence further pollutants either. Petrochemical exploration is a major cause of pollution in the polar region altering the polar bear's environment irreparably. Spillages and leakages of hydrocarbons, not to mention residues of heavy metals, acids, radio-active material, plastics and polystyrenes can additionally directly affect the environment as well as the insulating properties of the bear's fur leaving it vulnerable to hypothermia. Development of the Arctic landscape and disturbance by Man can also affect bear behaviour and denning.

Despite popular misconceptions, only 8 people have been killed by polar bears in the last 30 years in North America, often as a result of provocation. In an attempt to avoid potential conflicts between the residents and visitors to the township of Churchill (at the southern-most end of the polar bear's range, on the west coast of the Hudson Bay), a polar bear holding facility was established in 1982.

Churchill is the self-proclaimed polar bear capital of the world and base for polar bear-watching trips due to the concentration of bears it attracts in the summer months. When the ice has retreated and bears find the daily quest for food a challenge, they will naturally investigate easy pickings such as the local rubbish dump or kitchens for scraps. They quickly learn to take advantage of these sources and in turn can cause the human population some difficulty in going about their daily business. When a bear becomes a problem within the town, he/she is herded away from the town by specialised rangers.

'Problem' bears are usually inquisitive youngsters, around 3 or 4 years old, who are inexperienced foragers and are looking for easy pickings. Should the bear continue to enter the town it is captured (using a tranquilising drug) and placed in the bear holding facility (a cage-like structure able to contain upto 30 individuals) overnight from which it is transported, via helicopter, to a safe distance from the town. The opportunity of getting so close to a wild polar bear is never missed. Samples and measurements are taken from the bear for scientific analysis and it will be tagged and tattooed to aid future identification. These preventative measures have significantly reduced potential conflicts between the bears and the inhabitants of Churchill as well as gleaning valuable information which will go some way towards furthering our understanding of polar bears in the wild.

Scientific research of the polar bear has been on-going for around the past 30 years. The information it reveals about the species, its life and that of the rest of the Arctic ecosystem has never been more important in light of the threats the environment faces today. Only by understanding how polar bears live and survive on the frozen wastes of the Arctic can we, as humans, begin assess the extent of the effects we are having upon their habitat and help to ameliorate them. Although the majority of us will never see a polar bear in its natural habitat, it is our duty as custodians of the natural world to ensure that the polar bear does not become extinct as a result of our ignorance of different environments and certainly not within our immediate lifetimes or those of our grandchildren.

Opposite page: Female bear with year-old cubs.

Acknowledgements and Information

The authors / photographers of *Wildlife Monographs – Polar Bears* would like to thank the following in the capturing of these amazing images and the production of this book; Arne Kristoffersen, Rémy Marion, Evans Mitchell Books, the people of Churchill and Svalbard, Lynda & Merv Gunter of Tundra Buggy Adventures, Robert Buchanan (President, Polar Bears International). Mark Carwardine (for use of image of polar bear swimming, P36).

Conserving the polar bear

Due to the precarious current status of the polar bear and indications of rapid decline in productivity and survival, efforts are underway to attempt to reclassify the polar bear species as "vulnerable" under the international definitions of threatened world species. To facilitate the acquisition of detailed scientific information about the polar bear and its current and potential future status, several international organisations and charities are active in funding and supporting this vital scientific research.

Opposite page: We all affect the Arctic environment and ultimately the future of the polar bear.

Polar Bears International (PBI, www.polarbearsinternational.org) is one such charity dedicated to the cause of the polar bear and in educating people as to its needs and our effects upon it. As well as financially supporting crucial scientific studies such as assessments of denning areas based on the tundra and the effects of human impact in the Arctic regions; a major part of their work is in educating the general public about polar bears. The extensive educational programme includes provision for students to assist scientists in the field where they can gain hands-on experience of scientific procedures and disseminate their findings via live web broadcasts to schools and presentations to their peers.

Advances in modern technology have also helped PBI to set up a roving "polar bear cam" and remote cameras where you can watch the daily activities of bears in the Hudson Bay region. The PBI website provides a centralised hub of information and is the first point of contact should you wish to know about polar bears. Beyond the internet, the charity also organises series of lectures available to the general public including

residents in polar bear regions and eco-tourists. Scientific studies into the physiology and behaviour of polar bears in captivity are also supported, allowing us to glean vital information about polar bears that would be impossible to gain in the field as well as contributing to our understanding of the welfare needs of animals in captivity. By supporting such organisations as PBI we can all individually make a significant difference to the future of the polar bear in Arctic regions.

Where to see polar bears

By far the easiest place to view wild polar bears is at the self-proclaimed polar bear capital of the world at Churchill, Manitoba, Canada. There are numerous eco-tourism companies based here that offer trips to view polar bears and the other amazing local Arctic wildlife such as Gyr falcons, Arctic Hares and Arctic Foxes as well as other flora and fauna during the summer months such as Caribou and extensive birdlife. One of the most famous of operators is the Tundra Buggy® Adventure. Purpose-built vehicles, run on specialised floatation tyres to help minimize the vehicle's impact upon the fragile tundra environment, transport you close to bears as they congregate in anticipation of the reformation of sea ice at the end of the summer. There is nowhere else you can get as close to polar bears in relative comfort and in absolute safety, in the knowledge that your visit is as ecologically-friendly as possible. The tundra buggies have been running for 30 years and actively promote the conservation of polar bears and their scientific research.

Contact: Tundra Buggy® Adventure,
Frontiers North, Canada,
www.tundrabuggy.com

Photographic Notes

Photographing in extreme environments such as the biting cold of the Arctic, which at times can reach temperatures in excess of -40 °C, naturally limits what you are able to achieve. The weather conditions dictate exactly when, where and whether you can photograph polar bears at all. As such, the vast majority of the life of a polar bear is inaccessible to the prying lens.

Whether working in a film or digital format, the cold is a concern, mostly in relation to the rapid discharge of battery power. In order to keep your batteries lasting as long as possible, try to keep them warm. Have a replacement secreted next to your body, inside your jacket and ready to swap with a cold one, or ones that have been used up, at a moment's notice. Numerous hand warming packs are also very useful for keeping camera equipment warm and working.

Take care with your equipment when moving between outdoors and indoors after a day on the ice. Ensure that you place your equipment safely in a camera rucksack or bag (after removing batteries for re-charging) and seal it before entering a warm environment. Do not be tempted to open your bag and remove the equipment until it has warmed up gradually to the ambient temperature. Removing your equipment before it has had a chance to warm up, particularly lenses, will cause condensation on the glass and vital electronic components of the camera leaving you with fogged up lenses and potentially malfunctioning cameras.

Exposing a white subject on a white background can be tricky. Remember that the camera's built-in light meter will naturally wish to darken the image, so some positive compensation (usually in the range $+\frac{1}{2}$ to $+1$) may be required to make sure that the image is not under exposed.

Don't forget that if the weather or light is too poor for photography, simply put your camera down and enjoy the spectacle of watching polar bears!

Opposite page: Polar bear mother and cubs on frozen tundra.

Other wildlife titles published by

Evans Mitchell Books

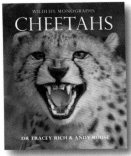

Wildlife Monographs
Cheetahs
ISBN: 978-1-901268-09-6

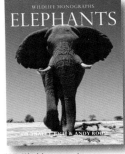

Wildlife Monographs
Elephants
ISBN: 978-1-901268-08-9

Wildlife Monographs
Giant Pandas
ISBN: 978-1-901268-13-3

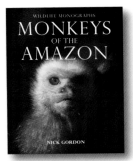

Wildlife Monographs
Monkeys of the Amazon
ISBN: 978-1-901268-10-2

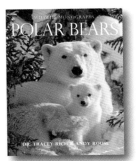

Wildlife Monographs
Polar Bears
ISBN: 978-1-901268-15-7

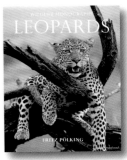

Wildlife Monographs
Loepards
ISBN: 978-1-901268-12-6

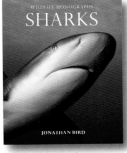

Wildlife Monographs
Sharks
ISBN: 978-1-901268-11-9

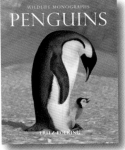

Wildlife Monographs
Penguins
ISBN: 978-1-901268-14-0

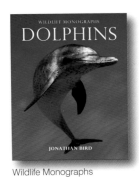

Wildlife Monographs
Dolphins
ISBN: 978-1-901268-17-1

Wildlife Monographs
Wolves
ISBN: 978-1-901268-18-8

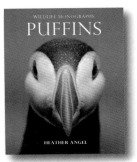

Wildlife Monographs
Puffins
ISBN: 978-1-901268-19-5